I'D LIKE TO THANK

... my beloved daughter **Jasmine** for brightening up every day of my life;

... my beloved husband and agent, **Stefan Lindström**, who has always believed in me and my crazy ideas;

... all the wonderful children who took part in this project and made this book possible;

... my editor, **Eva Stjerne**, for her efforts in getting my writing into shape;

... my dear brother, **Alan Maranik**, for giving this book a hugely appealing design—working with you is always such fun;

... **Christer Lindblom** at Stevali for helping me to get this book into bookstores in Sweden;

... **Ulf Kihlberg** at Bagaren och Kocken for the lovely glasses, mugs, pitchers, and fun gadgets from Rice, as well as the children's safety knives from MAC (www.bagarenochkocken.se); and finally

... **Carl Uggla** for the Vitamix blenders.

© Eliq Maranik and Stevali Production
Original title: *Smoothies för barn – upptäck, utforska, experimentera och lär dig allt om frukter och grönsaker*
ISBN 978-91-86287-71-9

Product idea, smoothies, and design: Eliq Maranik
Photos: Eliq Maranik
Art Director: Eliq Maranik
Layout: Eliq Maranik and Alan Maranik/Stevali Production
Editor: Eva Stjerne Ord & Form

© for the English edition: h.f.ullmann publishing GmbH
Translation from Swedish: Casper Sare in association with
First Edition Translations Ltd, Cambridge, UK
Coverphotos: Eliq Maranik
Overall responsibility for production: h.f.ullmann publishing
GmbH, Potsdam, Germany

Printed in Slovenia, 2016

ISBN 978-3-8480-0997-8
10 9 8 7 6 5 4 3 2 1
X IX VIII VII VI V IV III II I

www.ullmannmedien.com
info@ullmannmedien.com
facebook.com/hfullmann
twitter.com/hfullmann_int

Abbreviations and Quantities

1 oz = 1 ounce = 28 grams
1 lb = 1 pound = 16 ounces 1
1 cup = approx. 5–8 ounces* (see below)
1 cup = 8 fl uid ounces = 250 milliliters (liquids)
2 cups = 1 pint (liquids) = 15 milliliters (liquids)
8 pints = 4 quarts = 1 gallon (liquids)
1 g = 1 gram = 1/1000 kilogram = 5 ml (liquids)
1 kg = 1 kilogram = 1000 grams = 2¼ lb
I l = 1 liter = 1000 milliliters (ml) = 1 quart
125 milliliters (ml) = approx. 8 tablespoons = ½ cup
1 tbsp = 1 level tablespoon = 15–20 g* (depending on density) = 15 milliliters (liquids)
1 tsp = 1 level teaspoon = 3–5 g * (depending on density) = 5 ml (liquids)

*The weight of dry ingredients varies significantly depending on the density factor, e.g. 1 cup of flour weighs less than 1 cup of butter. Quantities in ingredients have been rounded up or down for convenience, where appropriate. Metric conversions may therefore not correspond exactly. It is important to use either American or metric measurements within a recipe. The purpose of the recipes and advice in this book is simply to give guidance on quality nutrition and how to increase your energy. If you have a medical condition you should consult your doctor.

Disclaimer

ELIQ MARANIK

SMOOTHIES FOR KIDS

h.f.ullmann

Contents

Getting started

Read this chapter before you start as it will make following recipes easier and safer. And do not forget to have loads of fun!

Safety first

The kitchen can be a dangerous place. Here are a few helpful things to keep in mind:

1. Get an adult to show you how to use the electrical appliances, knives, and other utensils you need. Make sure there is always an adult around the first few times you make a smoothie.

2. Let them know when you want to "make some mess" in the kitchen. It is good to have an adult nearby in case you need help.

3. Your hands should always be dry when you use electrical appliances. Do not forget to pull the plug out as soon as you are done.

4. Mind your fingers when cutting ingredients and never walk with a knife in your hand.

5. Never put your hands in the blender jar or the smoothie maker. The blades are really sharp and could do you serious harm. You should never poke the blade with, or place in the jar, anything that could damage the blender.

6. Always be careful when using hot water.

Hygiene

Hygiene is the second most important consideration after safety. Here are some ground rules:

1. Wash your hands, tie up your hair (if you need to do so), and put on an apron before you start.

2. Wash all fruits and berries, including the skin, because anything you touch could end up in the smoothie and then in your stomach.

3. Never use fruit that has soft spots or discolored patches, or visible bruises.

4. Always check the best-before date. Avoid using ingredients that are out of date.

5. Clean up after yourself and keep the kitchen looking tidy.

Here is how to make a smoothie

1. Read the recipe carefully before you start.
2. Make sure you have all the ingredients and equipment handy.
3. Chop the fruit into blender-size pieces.
4. Place the fruit in the blender.
5. Add the liquid to the blender.
6. Replace the cover, making sure it fits tightly.
7. Blend for 30 seconds to a minute.
8. Pour the smoothie into glasses, garnish, and serve.

The right tools for the job

BLENDER. You will need a blender to make smoothies. If you do not have a blender, you can use an immersion blender and the accompanying beaker, but a proper blender with a jar is much safer and easier to use, and you will have more fun using it. All you need to do is place all the ingredients in the jar, press the button, and then pour the smoothie into a glass. A smoothie maker is a type of blender that is safer for kids to use because it has a tap at the base of the jar.

CITRUS PRESS. A citrus press is a really handy tool when making smoothies. Be sure to wash it immediately after use because you will find it difficult to clean after the fruit pulp has dried on and stuck fast to it. Use a citrus press to juice all types of citrus fruits and even pomegranates.

CUTTING BOARD. Have a cutting board that you always use only for fruits and vegetables. It is really important that you wash your cutting board immediately after use. Otherwise, it might discolor, absorb food odors and flavors, or become a home for bacteria.

You will need **FREEZER BAGS** to freeze fruits and berries. Label them with the date, item name, and portion quantity for easy identification.

An **ICE-CREAM SCOOP** will come in handy when you make smoothies containing ice cream. Ice-cream scoops are made from strong material and will scoop really hard ice cream or frozen yogurt without bending. If you are finding it difficult, though, dip the scoop in some warm water before the first and between scoops.

ICE-CUBE TRAYS AND ICE-POP MOLDS. Those of you who want to freeze water, fruit juice, ice cream, or yogurt in fun-shape molds may want to invest in a variety of molds, available from kitchen supply stores or online. Another thing you can do is fill each hole of an ice-cube tray with berries, edible flowers, or herbs before pouring the liquid in, or freeze some scooped-out passion fruit pulp, fruit juice, or smoothie in your ice-pop molds.

KNIVES. You will need both small and large knives to chop fruit. You should have an adult nearby when you are using sharp knives. It is best to use a specially designed knife with a child-friendly grip, a non-slip handle, and a rounded tip.

SIEVES. Making extra-smooth smoothies is easy. Just strain them through a fine sieve to remove pieces of skin, seeds, and any other things you do not want in your smoothie. You can also sieve orange, grapefruit, lemon, and lime juice in order to remove the bitter pips. Consider using a nylon sieve when straining tart fruits because metal can spoil the flavor.

VEGETABLE PEELER. You will need a vegetable peeler to peel all hard-skinned fruits that are not organic, e.g. mangoes, apples, and pears. Be sure to wash them first.

Tips and tricks

Boosting flavor
If you think your smoothie is a little bit on the bland side, try adding some lemon or lime juice to boost the flavor. Some fruit, such as melons, mangoes, and bananas, can be a bit too sweet, so consider adding a little lemon juice to boost the fruitiness.

Thinning your smoothies
To thin out a smoothie that is too thick and mushy, add a little water, milk, sour milk, or juice. If you want the full flavor of the fruit to dominate, it is best to use water.

Thickening your smoothies
If your smoothie turns out too thin, try adding some crème fraîche, quark, cottage cheese, Greek yogurt, banana, avocado, or mango. You will get an even creamier consistency if you use ice cream or cream. Alternatively, try adding some tofu, muesli, nuts, or other fun and tasty food that is good for you.

Smoothing your smoothies
Some fruits and vegetables, such as apples, pears, and pineapples, are very high in fiber, which means they make smoothies rough textured and difficult to drink. You can press such a smoothie through a fine sieve before serving.

Making your smoothies frosty
To make frosty smoothies, it is best to use frozen fruits and berries. You could add plenty of ice, but that will make your smoothie taste less fruity and more watery. Remember that the ice will melt quickly if the smoothie is too warm in the first place. So be sure to chill your fruit to preserve all that lovely flavor.

Serve immediately
To get a full vitamin, flavor, and color blast, and for the best consistency, you should serve smoothies and fresh-pressed juices as soon as possible after preparing them. Homemade smoothies tend to change color and flavor very quickly, so it is best to drink them straightaway.

Smoothies for later

If you really want to save your smoothie for later, store it in a clean, stoppered glass bottle in the refrigerator. Since homemade smoothies do not contain any preservatives and since they are not pasteurized, you should not keep them in the fridge for more than 24 hours. After all, the vitamins begin to degrade straight after preparation and the smoothie can go off very quickly. The color, flavor, and consistency will change, too. Always give your smoothie a good shake before drinking it, and serve it with some nice berries or slices of fruit.

Smoothie pops

You can make your own ice pops with almost any fruit or berry smoothie. Look for inspiration among the recipes in this book, or make your own smoothies and pour them into ice-pop molds. To make striped ice pops—ice pops that combine different flavors and colors on the same stick—you need to freeze each smoothie layer for 30–45 minutes before pouring in the next one. Otherwise, the layers will blend. Do not store your pops in the freezer for longer than a week because they will become very icy and will not taste all that good anymore. Do not fill the molds all the way up to the top because the contents tend to swell a little in the freezer.

Create your own recipes

Get creative and dream up your own recipes. Basically, you can use any ingredients you like in a smoothie. Your imagination is the limit, so feel free to experiment.

Mild juices, such as those pressed from apples, pears, or carrots, or that pressed from an orange, combine well with most other fruits.

You are also welcome to use any dairy products, such as milk, sour milk, yogurt, quark, crème fraîche, cream, and cottage cheese. Just bear in mind that some ingredients contain a lot of fat and calories, and that they should not be eaten every day.

All types of ice cream, sorbet, frozen yogurt, juice, fruit, or berries are okay to use in frosty smoothies.

Garnishes

Do not forget the garnish! Serve your smoothies in style! Use beautiful glasses and garnish them with fresh berries, fruit, herbs, edible flowers, and other goodies. You can buy fun ice-pop molds, cocktail sticks and parasols, and similar drinks accessories in kitchen supply stores, or make your own. Alternatively, use those you have saved from vacations.

Lactose intolerance

If you are lactose intolerant, feel free to replace dairy with a lactose-free alternative: soy yogurt, soy ice cream, oat milk, or nut milk.

Taking smoothies to the next level

This chapter is for those of you who want to step up your smoothie-making skills.

Choose fruits and berries with care

Your smoothie will only be as tasty as the ingredients you put in it. So, use your eyes, your nose, your fingers to find the absolutely best fruit and vegetables at the produce counter, and choose organic and locally grown ingredients as much as possible. Organically grown fruit is completely free of additives, unsprayed, has a softer skin, and tastes so much better.

Take your time when choosing produce. Try to go for colorful, firm, fragrant fruits without any soft spots or discolored patches. Remember that picking produce yourself in a grocery store is better than buying it prepackaged.

Feel free to taste different varieties of apples, mangoes, melons, and other fruits. The flavor can vary enormously between varieties of the same fruit. One fun idea is to invite your family and friends to join you for some apple tasting.

Ripe or unripe

For best flavor and consistency, be sure to choose fruit that is just ripe enough. Unripe fruit is both tarter and harder, and lacks that little extra something. On the other hand, overripe fruit tends to be too sweet (and even may taste off, in fact), making the smoothie overly sweet. Choose fruit that feels heavy for its size and has a strong aroma: that is usually a sign of ripeness.

Once picked, most fruits ripen at room temperature. This makes some fruit taste sweeter and juicier with time, while other fruit may become juicier but not sweeter. Citrus fruits are one exception. Though picked when ripe, they become juicier if left on the countertop.

Washing fruits and berries

Unless you have a garden of your own, you simply will not have any way of knowing whether or not your fruit or berries have been treated, where they have been grown, or who has handled them. Most fruit, especially imported fruit, is sprayed to extend its shelf life. That is why it is really important that you thoroughly wash or rinse all fruit. Any fruit that is not organic should be peeled. Remember that everything that is on the surface of the fruit might end up in your digestive system.

The easiest way to clean hard-skinned fruits and vegetables thoroughly is to immerse them in lukewarm water and brush them with a soft vegetable brush. Use the brush for this purpose only and rinse it thoroughly after each use.

To clean soft fruits, rinse them in lukewarm water and then give them a gentle rub between your fingers. You can also clean them using the soft side of a scrub sponge, which you should use for that purpose only. Citrus fruits and fruits with a thick layer of wax can be washed with a little dish soap and a soft brush. Always remember to rinse the fruit thoroughly after using dish soap.

You should also thoroughly wash any fruit with an inedible skin—e.g. bananas, oranges, tangerines, melons, and mangoes—because the pesticides and wax will stick to your hands and end up in the flesh of the fruit.

To peel or not to peel?

Most vitamins, minerals, and enzymes are found just beneath the skin of the fruit, so be sure to leave the skin on as far as possible. If using only organic fruit and berries, in most cases you can leave the skin on when making smoothies or pressing juice. However, always be sure to first wash your fruits, berries, and vegetables thoroughly in lukewarm water. If using conventional fruit, remove as thin a layer of the skin/peel as possible.

Do be sure, though, to remove skins that are too hard because any small pieces of the skin will impair the smooth feel in your mouth. Bananas, mangoes, pineapples, papayas, and avocados should always be peeled.

Removing pits and pips

Most pits, pips, and seeds should be removed as they will make your smoothie bitter and gritty. Obviously, never place large or particularly hard pits, such as those of the nectarine, peach, plum, apricot, mango, avocado, and other stone fruits, in the blender jar. Dark seeds, especially those of the watermelon and passion fruit, will give your smoothie an unattractive color. Always be sure to de-seed papayas as the seeds have a peppery flavor.

Buying ready-to-eat frozen ingredients

Any fruits or berries frozen immediately after harvesting are a good alternative to fresh fruit. These days, you can find many different varieties in the store freezer aisles. Some grocery stores also sell ready-to-use freezer smoothie packs.

Freezing ingredients yourself

Although it is always best to use fresh fruits and berries, sometimes it can be a good idea to freeze them. Fresh strawberries, raspberries, and blueberries, for example, will keep only for a few days, so you should freeze them if you are planning to use them at a later date. Frozen fruits and berries can be added straight to the blender or defrosted before use.

It is usually a good idea to buy and freeze fruits, berries, and vegetables when they are in season. They will give the best taste to your smoothies and, besides, they tend to be better value when in season. Fruit will keep for two to three months in a regular freezer, but it can be stored for even longer periods at temperatures below 64 °F (18 °C).

Chop the fruits, berries, and vegetables just before you freeze them. Otherwise, you will quickly lose nutrients, vitamins, minerals, and enzymes to oxidation. Chop into blender-size pieces. Here is a tip: first freeze the individual pieces and then transfer them as individual portions into freezer bags, with one or more types of fruit and berries in each. Use airtight freezer bags and try to remove as much air from the bags as possible before sealing them. Always label your bags with the date, item name, and portion quantity. Finally, keep in mind that any leftover juice can be frozen in ice-cube trays and stored in the same way. It makes a perfect addition to smoothies!
Fruits and berries that freeze well: bananas, blackberries, blueberries, cherries, cranberries, currants, mangoes, papayas, pineapple, raspberries, rhubarb, and strawberries.

Fruits and berries that become watery and mushy when frozen: apples, apricots, citrus fruits, grapes, kiwis, nectarines, peaches, pears, and plums.

Sea buckthorn, mango, and strawberry

SERVES 2

1 fresh mango (or 1½ cups / 300 g frozen mango chunks)

1 cup / 100 g sea buckthorn, fresh or frozen (or 2 tsp sea buckthorn powder)

8–10 strawberries, fresh or frozen

generous ¾ cup / 200 ml

fresh-pressed apple juice

generous ¾ cup / 200 ml water

a few ice cubes (if you use only fresh fruit)

1. Wash all the fresh fruits thoroughly.

2. Peel the mango with a vegetable peeler and chop it into small chunks. Keep in mind that there is a hard pit inside, so be extra careful. Get help from an adult if you are finding it difficult.

3. Place the chopped mango and sea buckthorn in the blender.

4. Hull the strawberries (if you use fresh) and add them to the blender. You may want to reserve a few for the garnish.

5. Pour in the apple juice and water, and blend it all to a smooth consistency. For a frostier consistency, add a few ice cubes.

6. Serve in large glasses with a straw and garnish with a few strawberries or sea buckthorn berries.

Did you know that...

... a single small sea buckthorn berry is said to contain as much vitamin C as a whole orange?

... sea buckthorn contains vitamin B12, which very rarely occurs in plants and is particularly important for vegetarians?

... sea buckthorn is a dioecious plant, meaning that there are separate male and female plants? The female plant will not produce berries before it has been pollinated by a male plant. Male plants have also been found to produce berries, but not as many as the female ones.

Blueberry, raspberry, and herbal tea

SERVES 2

generous ¾ cup / 200 ml herbal tea

2 tsp dried goji berries

6 dates, pitted

generous 1 cup / 150 g blueberries, frozen

1½ cups / 150 g raspberries, frozen

Did you know that...

... blueberries are rich in anti-oxidants and they are sometimes called superberries? Bilberries (wild blueberries) are said to be particularly nutritious.

1. Make the herbal tea. Steep two bags of herbal tea in 1¼ cups / 300 ml hot water. Leave to steep for 10–15 minutes and take out the tea bags, pressing them between two spoons to get as much liquid out as possible. Leave the tea to cool, then chill thoroughly in the refrigerator. Get help from an adult if you are finding it difficult.

2. Place the tea, goji berries, and dates in the blender. Leave to stand for 5–10 minutes, until the goji berries soften.

3. Add the frozen berries, saving a few for the garnish.

4. Blend it all into a frosty, wholesome smoothie.

5. Garnish with fresh or frozen berries. Serve with thick straws.

Spinach and pineapple

2–3 cups / 50–100 g fresh spinach (to taste)

1 lime

1 banana

½ cup / 100 g pineapple, frozen

1¼ cups / 300 ml

fresh-pressed apple juice

1. Wash the spinach well and leave to dry. Reserve a few leaves for the garnish.

2. Wash all the fresh fruits thoroughly. Place them in the blender.

3. Cut the lime in half, and juice each half using a citrus press. Be sure to strain out all the pips, otherwise the smoothie will have a bitter taste.

4. Add the lime juice and the remaining ingredients to the blender and blend to a smooth consistency.

5. For a frostier consistency, add a few ice cubes.

6. Serve in large glasses with a straw, and garnish with the reserved spinach leaves.

Did you know that...

... spinach is a superfood? Its leaves are incredibly nutritious and high in antioxidants?

... there is a comic strip in which Popeye the Sailor Man eats loads of spinach to gain strength.

Piña chocolada

½ pineapple (approx. 1½ cups / 300 g), fresh or frozen

generous ¾ cup / 200 ml water

generous ¾ cup / 200 ml coconut milk (additive free)

5 dates, pitted

2 tbsp cold-pressed coconut oil

3 tbsp cacao powder

a few ice cubes (if you use fresh pineapple)

coconut flakes for the garnish

1. If you use fresh pineapple, wash it thoroughly.

2. If you are finding it difficult, ask an adult to cut off the leaves and the hard skin. Alternatively, use frozen pineapple, which is simpler.

3. If you use fresh pineapple, chop it into small chunks.

4. Place all the ingredients except the ice cubes in the blender and blend to a smooth consistency.

5. Blend in the ice cubes if you use fresh pineapple or if you want a frosty smoothie.

6. Serve in pretty tumblers and sprinkle some coconut flakes on top.

Did you know that...

... the coconut palm tree blossoms up to 13 times a year, and the nuts can therefore be harvested all year round? Each coconut tree yields an average of sixty fruits a year, which means 10,000 fruits during its lifetime. The coconut tree gives us coconut oil, coconut water, coconut milk, coconut palm sugar, coconut flour, coconut nectar, coconut vinegar, coconut chips, coconut flakes, and much more.

Did you know that...

... coconut oil is one of the healthiest oils in the world? Solid at room temperature, coconut oil becomes a liquid at 75 °F (24 °C).
... coconut oil is suitable for cooking, smoothies, and desserts, as well as for body care products—e.g. skin moisturizer or lip balm?
... you should always buy organic, raw, cold-pressed coconut oil? The label should read: "100 percent coconut."

Mango, raspberry, and passion fruit

SERVES 2

2 mangoes (or 3 cups / 600 g frozen chunks)

5 passion fruits (or 2–3 tsp passion fruit powder)

½ lime

1½ cups / 150 g raspberries, frozen

generous ¾ cup / 200 ml ice-cold water

a few ice cubes (if you use fresh mango)

Did you know that...

...originally, the mango grew only in the mountainous regions of the Himalayas, and that people in India and Myanmar started growing it several thousand years ago?

... the mango tree can grow to a height of 115–130 feet (35–40 m) and that it has a huge crown?

... the flowers of the mango tree have a lily fragrance? It takes three to six months for the fruits to ripen after blossoming. The skin of the mango shifts in color from yellow to orange to red.

... you can freeze mango in plastic bags when it is in season? It is better both in terms of price and taste than eating mangoes that have been picked unripe, stored for long periods, and sprayed with various agents so they keep for months. Fresh, newly harvested fruit is always your best option, but newly harvested fruit that has been frozen straightaway will be just fine.

1. Wash all the fruits thoroughly.

2. Peel the mango with a vegetable peeler and chop it into small chunks. Keep in mind that there is a hard pit inside, so be extra careful. Get help from an adult if you are finding it difficult.

3. Place the mango chunks in the blender.

4. Cut the passion fruits in half. Reserve one half for the garnish. Scoop out the pulp of the other halves, straining off the seeds (if you wish).

5. Cut the lime in half, and juice one half using a citrus press. Strain out all the pips, as otherwise the smoothie will have a bitter taste.

6. Add the raspberries, lime juice, and water to the blender, and blend it all to a smooth consistency. For a frostier smoothie, add a few ice cubes.

7. If you like, you can strain the smoothie for a smoother consistency before serving.

8. Serve in large glasses and decorate with the pulp from the remaining passion fruit.

TIP

The easiest way to separate the seeds of the passion fruit from the pulp is to pour a little water into each half and stir until the pulp loosens. This allows you to strain the pulp and use only the tasty liquid in your smoothie.

Strawberries, goji berries, and chamomile

SERVES 2

1¼ cup / 300 ml chamomile tea

2 tbsp dried goji berries

½ lemon

12 strawberries, fresh or frozen

1 banana

2 tsp honey (or 2 tbsp agave syrup)

1. Make the chamomile tea, using two teabags in 1¼ cup (300 ml) of hot water. Leave to steep for 10–15 minutes, then remove the tea bags, squeezing out as much liquid as possible between two spoons. Leave the tea to cool down and place in the refrigerator to go cold. Get help from an adult if you are finding it difficult.

2. Pour the tea into a blender and add the goji berries, leaving them to soak and soften for 5–10 minutes.

3. Meanwhile, thoroughly rinse all the fresh fruit.

4. Cut the lemon in half, juice one half, and pour it into the blender.

5. Hull the strawberries, if you use fresh ones.

6. Add the strawberries to the blender, reserving two for the garnish.

7. Peel and chop the banana, and add it to the blender.

8. Pour in the honey or agave syrup, and blend.

9. Garnish each smoothie glass with the reserved strawberry.

Did you know that...

... chamomile grows in the wild, in fields, and along roads, and that it is one of the world's oldest and most widely used medicinal plants? It is picked primarily for its flowers.

... dried or fresh chamomile flowers are usually used for tea? Use 1–2 tsp dried flowers to make a large cup of tea. The tea is good for stomach pain and is soothing for those who have trouble falling asleep at night.

... you should avoid chamomile if you are allergic to plants in the daisy family?

Peanut chocolate

2 bananas

3 tbsp peanut butter

2 tbsp cacao powder

1¾ cups /400 ml water

natural peanuts for garnish

1. Wash, peel, and chop the bananas, then freeze them for a couple of hours. Frozen banana will ensure an ice-cream consistency, so you will not need to use ice.

2. Place all the ingredients in the blender and blend to an ice-creamy consistency.

3. Serve in pretty tumblers and garnish with crushed natural peanuts.

Did you know that...

... peanuts are not actually nuts, but legumes, and that they are related to peas, beans, lentils, soybeans, and garbanzo beans?

... people with an allergy to peanuts may react very strongly to them? That is why eating peanuts is not recommended in crowded places—e.g. buses, schools, movie theaters, etc.

... good-quality peanut butter should be organic and contain at least 99 percent peanuts, and perhaps a little sea salt? That and nothing else. Unsalted peanut butter is best for smoothies. Never buy peanut butter that contains palm oil and sugar!

Rose hip, pineapple, and papaya

SERVES 2

¼ fresh pineapple (or 1 cup / 200 g frozen pineapple chunks)

juice of ½ lemon

¾ cup / 150 g papaya, frozen

3 tsp rose-hip powder (dried, ground rose hips)

generous ¾ cup / 200 ml fresh-pressed apple juice

7 tbsp / 100 ml water

a few ice cubes (if you use fresh pineapple)

1. Wash all the fresh fruits thoroughly.

2. Remove the leaves and the hard skin from the pineapple. Get help from an adult if you are finding it difficult, or use frozen pineapple, which is simpler.

3. Chop the pineapple into small chunks and put it in the blender.

4. Add the juice of half a lemon to the blender.

5. Add the remaining ingredients, except the ice cubes, to the blender and blend to a smooth consistency. For a frostier consistency, add ice cubes.

6. Serve in large glasses with a straw and garnish with rose-hip powder or fresh rose-hip berries.

Did you know that...

... in the past people used to eat rose hips to fight scurvy, i.e. vitamin C deficiency? Sometimes, rose hips were also given to horses in order to improve their immunity.

... the powder of whole rose-hip berries is made of whole, dried rose hips, and it contains sixty times more vitamin C than citrus fruits? In addition, rose hips are rich in antioxidants and essential minerals.

... it is very easy to make rose-hip powder yourself? You just need to dry whole berries and grind them to a powder using a coffee grinder.

What is the immune system?

The immune system is one of the body's most advanced systems. It serves to protect us from attack by viruses and bacteria.

In many countries three out of four people get a cold at least once a year. There are about two hundred kinds of cold virus out there at any given time. It is important to have strong immunity that will protect us from common colds, and from serious infections and diseases.

You can strengthen your immunity by eating plenty of fruit and vegetables, and by drinking smoothies.

Blackberry, vanilla yogurt, and cinnamon

2 cups / 200 g blackberries, fresh or frozen

5 dates, pitted

generous ¾ cup / 200 ml fresh-pressed apple juice

generous ¾ cup / 200 g vanilla yogurt

1 tsp ground cinnamon

2 tbsp shelled hemp seeds (optional)

a few ice cubes (if you use fresh blackberries)

1. Wash all the fruits thoroughly.
2. Place all the ingredients in the blender and blend to a smooth consistency.
3. For a frostier consistency, add a few ice cubes.
4. Garnish with a few blackberries.

Did you know that...

... a handful of blackberries contains almost half your daily requirement of fiber? Fiber keeps the bowels moving and facilitates digestion.

... blackberries belong to the same genus as raspberries, and that, just like raspberries, they are made up of lots of tiny segments (called drupelets) that contain a small seed?

Apricot, raspberry, and chamomile

SERVES 2

1¼ cup / 300 ml chamomile tea

10 apricots, fresh or dried

2 tbsp goji berries

½ lime

2 cups / 200 g raspberries, frozen

1. Make the chamomile tea, using two teabags in 1¼ cup (300 ml) of hot water. Leave to steep for 10–15 minutes, then remove the tea bags, squeezing out as much liquid as possible between two spoons. Leave the tea to cool, then chill thoroughly in the refrigerator. Get help from an adult if you are finding it difficult.

2. Pour the tea into a blender and add the apricots and goji berries, leaving them to soak and soften for 10-15 minutes. If you use fresh apricots, be sure to first wash and cut them in half, and then carefully remove the pits.

3. Cut the lime in half, juice one half, and pour the juice into the blender.

4. Add the frozen raspberries to the blender, reserving some for the garnish.

5. Blend it all to a yummy smoothie.

6. Garnish with an apricot or a raspberry. Serve!

Did you know that...

... the apricot is called *Prunus armeniaca*, which means Armenian plum, in Latin? But, we now know that the fruit is actually native to China, where it was grown as early as 4,000–5,000 years ago. These days, almost the entire world's apricot production takes place in Turkey.

... you can use dried apricots (preferably organic) as getting hold of fresh ones can be difficult? Just be sure to soak them for a while before use.

Pecan, date, and coconut water

SERVES 2

½ cup / 50 g pecans, natural

generous ¾ cup / 200 ml coconut water

1 tbsp shelled chia seeds (optional)

6 dates, pitted

2 bananas, sliced and frozen

1 tbsp cacao powder

1 tsp ground cardamom

1. Soak the pecans for a few hours or overnight. Reserve a few for the garnish.

2. Rinse the pecans and place them in the blender along with the coconut water, chia seeds, and dates. Blend them to a creamy consistency.

3. Then, blend in the frozen banana, cacao powder, and cardamom.

4. Serve in pretty tumblers and garnish with a few pecans.

Did you know that...

... coconut water is the clear liquid found in young, green coconuts? Coconut water is 95 percent water, the remainder consisting of nutrients and minerals. Coconut water is particularly rich in potassium and is sometimes called "nature's own sports drink."

... coconut water is not the same thing as coconut milk, which is made from the white flesh of a ripe, brown coconut?

... coconut water freezes well in ice-cube trays and keeps for six months in the freezer?

... chia seeds are a true superfood? Two teaspoons of chia seeds contain more omega 3 fatty acid than a regular-size salmon fillet. The omega 3 fatty acid is important for the body's hormonal balance and is said to have an anti-inflammatory effect.

Chocolate, coconut, and date

SERVES 2

2 bananas, fresh or frozen

5 dates, pitted

generous ¾ cup / 200 ml coconut milk (additive free)

2 tbsp cold-pressed coconut oil

2 tbsp cacao powder

1 tsp cinnamon, ground

generous ¾ cup / 200 ml water

a few ice cubes (if you use fresh bananas)

coconut flakes for the garnish

1. Rinse, peel, and slice the bananas.

2. Put all the ingredients except the ice cubes in the blender, and blend to a smooth consistency.

3. Blend in the ice cubes if you use fresh bananas or if you want a frosty smoothie.

4. Serve in pretty tumblers and sprinkle some coconut flakes on top.

Did you know that...

... dates are the fruits of the date palm? The date palm can grow to up to 115 feet (35 m) tall. It grows in the oases of the Middle East and North Africa, and also in the south of Europe, where it is not so common a sight.

... dates have been grown for more than 8,000 years? There are more than 1,500 varieties.

... the date fruit has an elongated berry shape and that it comes in many different sizes and colors? The smallest measures only about 1 inch (2.5 cm) in length, the longest about 2¾ inches (7 cm).

... ripe dates may be dark brown, reddish, or yellowish brown? The riper dates are, the sweeter they become. Dried dates are the sweetest.

Blueberry, blackberry, and red beet

SERVES 2

1 mini red beet, raw

1¼ cups / 300 ml fresh-pressed apple juice

generous 1½ cups / 200 g blueberries, frozen

1 cup / 100 g blackberries, frozen

1. Wash, peel, and chop the red beet into small chunks. Alternatively, you can use 7 tbsp / 100 ml fresh-pressed red beet juice—if so, skip to the next step.

2. Blend the red beet with the apple juice until you achieve an even, smooth consistency.

3. Add the frozen berries and blend to a frosty consistency.

Did you know that...

... red beet cleanses the blood and promotes the growth of red blood cells?

... there is a variety of red beet (the candy cane beet) whose exterior resembles the regular beet, but whose interior has a striped candy cane pattern?

Tropical fruit

½ cup / 100 g papaya, frozen

½ cup / 100 g pineapple, frozen

½ cup / 100 g mango, frozen

2 tsp dried goji berries

1¼ cups / 300 ml coconut water

2 tbsp coconut milk

1. Remove the fruit from the freezer and leave to defrost partly.

2. Leave the goji berries to soak and soften in the coconut water for 5–10 minutes.

3. Place all the ingredients in the blender and blend to a frosty consistency.

4. Garnish with a few goji berries.

TIP

Feel free to replace the frozen fruits with another type of tropical fruit mix.

Did you know that...

... goji berries contain five hundred times more vitamin C than an orange, three times more iron than spinach, and four times more antioxidants than cherries? Goji berries may be eaten fresh or dried, or drunk as a juice.

Pomegranate and grapefruit

2 pomegranates

2 pink grapefruit

2 oranges

½ cup / 100 g mango, frozen

1. Wash all the fresh fruits thoroughly.

2. Cut the pomegranates in half and juice the seeds from each half using a citrus press, just as you would an orange. You can include the pomegranate seeds if you want to get extra fiber.

3. Cut the grapefruit in half and juice each half using a citrus press.

4. Blend the juices with the frozen mango until you reach a smooth consistency.

5. Serve with a few pomegranate seeds as a garnish.

Did you know that...

... you can buy fresh pomegranates during the winter months? When they are not available, you can use frozen or dried pomegranate seeds.

... pomegranate is a superfruit and that it has been grown for thousands of years?

How do you de-seed a pomegranate?

Are you struggling to remove those tasty seeds from the pomegranate? Here is a tip: roll the fruit first against a hard surface to loosen the seeds, and then cut it in half. Holding each half face-down over a bowl in one hand, tap the skin with a wooden spoon and—abracadabra—watch the seeds fall out!

Raspberry and pear

SERVES 2

3 ripe pears

2 cups / 200 g raspberries, frozen

7 tbsp / 100 ml fresh-pressed apple juice

generous ¾ cup / 200 ml ice-cold water

sweetener of your choice

1. Cut the pears into quarters and remove the cores.

2. Blend the pears with raspberries, apple juice, and water to a smooth consistency—the harder the pears, the longer they will take to blend. Taste the blended mixture and add the sweetener to taste. Garnish with a few reserved raspberries.

Did you know that...

... pears contain twice as much fiber as apples?

... pears have a short shelf life? What you can do is buy unripe pears and place them in the refrigerator for a few days before eating them.

... if you want to speed up the ripening process you can place pears in a paper bag along with an apple? Apples produce ethylene gas, which makes fruit ripen faster.

Watermelon and raspberry

SERVES 2

¼ medium-size watermelon (about 2 cups / 400 g)

2 cups / 200 g raspberries, frozen

½ lime

1 tsp vanilla sugar

Ice cubes (optional)

a few slices of watermelon as a snack

1. Wash the watermelon thoroughly, getting help from an adult if it is too heavy to manage.

2. Carefully cut the watermelon into quarters with a knife. Remove the seeds from one of the quarters, scoop out the flesh, and place in the blender.

3. Add the frozen raspberries to the blender.

4. Wash the lime, cut it in half, and juice each half straight into the blender jar. Do not drop any pips in as they will make your smoothie taste bitter. Add the sugar.

5. Blend it all to a frosty smoothie. For an even frostier consistency, add a few ice cubes.

6. Enjoy the smoothie with the remaining watermelon slices as a snack.

TIP

If you roll the lime very firmly between your hands or against a flat surface, the flesh inside will soften and you will find it easier to extract all the juice. You can use a citrus press instead of squeezing the lime halves with your hand.

Did you know that...

... according to Guinness World Records, the largest watermelon ever weighed 268.80 pounds / 121.93 kg? It was grown in Arkansas, USA, in 2005.

... you can tell whether the watermelon is ripe without cutting into it? Knock on it with your knuckles. If it sounds hollow, it is ripe.

... watermelons are more than 90 percent water?

Lingonberry, pear, and orange

SERVES 2

2 oranges

2 tbsp dried goji berries

2 ripe pears

2 cups / 200 g lingonberries, fresh or frozen

a few ice cubes (if you use fresh berries)

honey (optional)

1. Juice the oranges.

2. Leave the goji berries to soak and soften in the orange juice for 5–10 minutes.

3. Cut the pears into quarters and remove the cores.

4. Blend all the ingredients except the ice cubes to a smooth consistency.

5. Blend in the ice for a frosty smoothie.

6. Taste the blended mixture and sweeten with honey, if desired. Garnish with a few lingonberries.

Did you know that...

... lingonberries kill bacteria and that they are just as good as cranberries against urinary tract infections?

... in the past lingonberries used to be sold in pharmacies, as a medicine against fever, among other uses?

TIP

If you can't get hold of fresh or frozen lingonberries, try to get freeze-dried lingonberry powder from a health food store. You can substitute cranberries for lingonberries.

Mango and saffron

1½ cups / 300 g mango, frozen

1 orange

1 lime

1½ cups / 400 g vanilla yogurt

half a pack of saffron (approx. 3 threads or 0.25 g)

1. Wash all the fresh fruits thoroughly.

2. Cut the orange and lime in half and juice them using a citrus press. Be sure to strain out all the pips, otherwise the smoothie will have a bitter taste.

3. Transfer the juices, frozen mango chunks, yogurt, and saffron into the blender jar, and blend to a frosty, golden-colored smoothie.

4. Garnish with mango. Serve with jumbo smoothie straws.

Did you know that...

... saffron is the world's most expensive spice and one that is most commonly adulterated?

... saffron is made from the stigmas of the crocus flower, which are picked and cleaned by hand? You need the stigmas of 110,000–170,000 flowers to make 2.2 pounds / 1 kg of dried saffron.

... saffron is used as a dye, spice, and fragrance, and that it is also used medicinally?

... saffron is toxic in large quantities, so you should not eat too much of it? The recommended maximum daily "dose" is 0.05 oz / 1.5 g, which is equivalent to 3 whole packs of saffron.

Kiwi and banana

SERVES 2

4 kiwis

2 bananas

7 tbsp / 100 ml fresh-pressed apple juice

6 tbsp / 100 g Turkish/Greek yogurt

4 ice cubes

1. Wash all the fruits thoroughly.

2. Peel and slice the kiwis and bananas. Reserve a few kiwi slices with the skin on for the garnish. Place everything else in the blender.

3. Blend it all to a smooth consistency, but be sure you do not blend for too long. If you overblend, the small kiwi seeds will add a very bitter and astringent flavor to the smoothie.

4. Pour into glasses and serve with a kiwi slice.

Did you know that...

... according to Guinness World Records, the record time for peeling and eating a kiwi is 5.35 seconds?

... a kiwi contains five times more vitamin C than an orange, as well as plenty of fiber?

... you can eat the skin of the kiwi?! If you do, be sure to first wash it thoroughly.

... the kiwi fruit is named after the New Zealand bird called a kiwi, which has a similar appearance?

Strawberry and pineapple

SERVES 2

¼ medium-size pineapple or 1 cup / 200 g frozen pineapple chunks

3 cups / 300 g strawberries, fresh or frozen

1 banana

generous ¾ cup / 200 ml ice-cold water

1. Wash all the fresh fruits thoroughly.

2. Get help from an adult if you are using a fresh pineapple. Cut the pineapple in half lengthwise, then cut one half into half again. Cut off the leaves, skin, and hard core, chop into chunks, and place in the blender. Freeze the leftover pineapple.

3. Hull the strawberries, if you use fresh ones. Reserve two strawberries for the garnish. adding the remainder to the blender.

4. Peel and chop the banana, and add it to the blender with the water.

5. Blend it all to a smooth consistency. If you like, you can strain the smoothie for a smoother consistency before serving.

6. Pour into glasses and serve with a strawberry.

Did you know that...
... fresh strawberries are best kept unhulled in a cool spot? If hulled, they should be eaten immediately or frozen.
... you should leave on the green leafy tops when washing strawberries, so that the berries retain their flavor?

TIP
This smoothie is perfect for freezing in ice-pop molds! For more details, please see page 14.

Blackberry and quark

2 cups / 200 g blackberries, fresh or frozen

1 banana

generous ¾ cup / 200 g natural yogurt

generous ¾ cup / 200 g vanilla quark

4 ice cubes (if you use fresh blackberries)

1. Wash the blackberries thoroughly if you use fresh ones and leave to dry.

2. Wash, peel, and slice the banana, and place it in the blender.

3. Add the blackberries to the blender. Reserve a few for the garnish.

4. Add the natural yogurt and vanilla quark.

5. Blend it all to a smooth and viscous consistency.

6. Serve with a few blackberries as a garnish.

Did you know that...

... blackberries, just like raspberries, are made up of lots of tiny segments (called drupelets) that contain a small seed? All those small seeds add fiber to your diet.

... blackberries taste really bad if they are eaten too early in the season? Leave them to ripen properly before picking them. Most blackberries will not ripen until fall.

Raspberry and nectarine

SERVES 2

3 nectarines (or peaches)

2 cups / 200 g raspberries, fresh or frozen

½ banana

7 tbsp / 100 ml fresh-pressed apple juice

7 tbsp / 100 ml ice-cold water

1. Wash all the fresh fruits thoroughly.

2. Carefully remove the pits from the nectarines. Keep in mind that the pit is hard, so be extra careful. Get help from an adult if you are finding it difficult.

3. Cut the nectarines into small chunks and place in the blender.

4. Add the fresh or frozen raspberries to the blender, reserving some for the garnish.

5. Peel and slice the banana in half and add to the blender.

6. Pour in the apple juice and water, and blend it all to a smooth consistency. If you like, you can strain the smoothie for a smoother consistency before serving.

7. Garnish with a raspberry on a cocktail stick. Serve!

Did you know that...

... peaches and nectarines are full of vitamin C and that they are rich in potassium and fiber? They also contain beta-carotene, which the body converts to vitamin A. Vitamin A is essential for good eyesight.

... the nectarine is the same fruit as the peach, only a "bald" variety? The nectarine has a soft, smooth skin, while the peach has a downy, velvety one.

... peaches and nectarines can grow on the same tree?

Strawberry and meringue peaks

SERVES 2

2 cups / 200 g strawberries, fresh or frozen

generous ¾ cup milk / 200 ml milk

3 tbsp crème fraîche

6 small meringues

1. Wash and hull the strawberries.

2. Blend the strawberries, milk, and crème fraîche to a smooth consistency.

3. Pour into the glasses, crumbling 2 meringues into each glass.

4. Stir with a spoon and crumble in the remaining meringues.

5. Serve!

TIP
You can buy ready-to-eat meringues, but you can also make your own.

How much milk does a cow produce?

A good dairy cow produces about 6.6 gallons / 25 liters of milk a day and is milked two to three times a day. That is roughly 2,377 gallons / 9,000 liters of milk every year. For a cow to produce milk, she must first give birth to a calf. The cow has to be milked regularly and farmers must be sure they do not stop milking, otherwise she will quickly develop a lot of pain in her udder and get mastitis (inflammation of the udder).

Banana and yogurt

2 ripe bananas

generous ¾ cup / 200 g vanilla yogurt

generous ¾ cup milk / 200 ml milk

2 tsp confectioner's sugar

1. Wash, peel, and slice the bananas, and place them in the blender.

2. Add the yogurt, milk, and confectioner's sugar.

3. Blend it all to a smooth consistency.

4. Pour into glasses. If desired, you can top the smoothies with a few banana chunks. Serve!

Did you know that...

... bananas grow on above-ground stems and that sometimes one such stem has up to two hundred bananas on it? The banana is not only a fruit, but a herb and a berry.

... the banana is one of the few fruits that you can't extract juice from? When making a banana-based smoothie, you always need to add some liquid. The sweet flavor and thick consistency of the banana makes tart and watery smoothies more filling and tasty.

TIP

If you want an ice-cold smoothie, freeze your bananas in advance. To do so, simply peel and slice the bananas approx. ¾ in / 2 cm thick. Transfer the slices onto a tray or plate, being careful not to overcrowd them, and leave in the freezer for a few hours or overnight. If you do not use up all the banana, transfer the frozen slices into a plastic bag and seal well so that the bag is airtight. Put them in the freezer. That is also a good way to store bananas that have started to become overripe. That way, you do not have to throw them away. Frozen banana is an excellent ingredient in smoothies.

Raspberry and vanilla

SERVES 2

2 cups / 200 g raspberries, fresh or frozen

1 ripe banana

6 tbsp / 100 g vanilla yogurt

generous ¾ cup milk / 200 ml milk

1 tsp vanilla sugar

honey (optional)

1. Wash the raspberries thoroughly, if you use fresh ones, and leave to dry.

2. Wash, peel, and slice the banana, and place it in the blender.

3. Add the raspberries to the blender, reserving some for the garnish.

4. Add the remaining ingredients.

5. Blend them all to a smooth and viscous consistency.

6. Taste the blended mixture and sweeten with honey, if desired.

7. Serve!

Did you know that...

... a raspberry is made up of lots of tiny segments (called drupelets) that each contain a small seed?

... raspberries are rich in vitamin C and fiber?

... raspberries can be stored for no more than two days in the refrigerator, but freeze just fine? In the freezer, they will keep for three to four months.

Blueberry and vanilla ice cream

3 cups / 300 g blueberries, fresh or frozen

6 tbsp / 100 g natural yogurt

generous ¾ cup milk / 200 ml milk

3 scoops vanilla ice cream

1. Wash the blueberries thoroughly, if you use fresh ones, and leave to dry.

2. Place two thirds in the blender. Reserve the rest for the garnish.

3. Add the natural yogurt, milk, and 3 scoops of vanilla ice cream to the blender.

4. Blend it all to a smooth consistency.

5. Pour into glasses and sprinkle the remaining blueberries on top. Serve!

Did you know that...

... in the USA, blueberries are second only to strawberries in popularity among berries? They have high antioxidant properties too.

... a blueberry shrub needs about fifteen years to grow to full height? A blueberry shrub can reach the age of several hundred years.

... blueberries, along with several other berries, are the staple food source for bears, and that they supply almost half of a bear's annual energy needs? Every day, a bear can eat a third of its weight in blueberries.

TIP

If you want your smoothie to have more of an ice-cream consistency, use frozen blueberries and substitute two extra scoops of ice cream for the yogurt. Eat with a spoon.

Mango and orange

1 mango

½ banana

3 oranges or 1¼ cups / 300 ml fresh-pressed orange juice

ice cubes (optional)

1. Wash all the fruits thoroughly.

2. Peel the mango with a vegetable peeler and chop it into small chunks. Keep in mind that there is a hard pit inside, so be extra careful. Get help from an adult if you are finding it difficult. Reserve a few mango slices for the garnish.

3. Place the mango chunks in the blender.

4. Peel and slice the half banana and add to the blender.

5. Cut the oranges in half and juice them using a citrus press. Be sure to remove all the pips as, otherwise, the smoothie will have a bitter taste.

6. Pour in the orange juice and blend it all to a smooth consistency. For an even frostier consistency, add a few ice cubes.

7. Serve topped with mango slices on a toothpick or cocktail stick.

Did you know that...

... according to Guinness World Records, the heaviest mango ever weighed 7.6 pounds / 3.43 kg, which is equivalent to a smallish watermelon? A regular size mango weighs 0.9–1.1 pounds / 400–500 g.

... India grows more than half of the world's mangoes?

... the fruit of the mango belongs to the same family as cashew nuts and pistachios? People with allergies should be careful around mangoes, at least when handling the skin.

Pineapple and carrot

SERVES 2

¼ medium-size pineapple or 1 cup / 200 g frozen pineapple chunks

4 strawberries, fresh or frozen

½ lime

generous ¾ cup / 200 ml fresh-pressed carrot juice

1. Wash all the fresh fruits thoroughly.
2. Get help from an adult if you are using a fresh pineapple. Cut the pineapple in half lengthwise, then cut one half into half again. Cut off the leaves, skin, and hard core; chop into chunks, and place it in the blender. Chop the leftover pineapple into chunks and place in a freezer bag.
3. Hull the strawberries, if you use fresh ones, and add them to the blender.
4. Cut the lime in half. Juice one half with a citrus press and add to the blender. Be sure to strain out all the pips.
5. Add the fresh-pressed carrot juice to the blender.
6. Blend it all to a smooth consistency. For an even smoother consistency, you can strain the smoothie before pouring it into glasses.
7. Serve!

EXPERIMENT

The carrot is a root that absorbs water from the soil, but how does the water reach the green tops?

For this experiment, you will need:

1 carrot, with tops on

1 glass of water

red food coloring

water

Method: Fill the glass halfway up with water. Drip in ten drops of the red food coloring. Cut off the tip of the carrot and place the carrot in the water. Place the glass with the carrot on a sunny windowsill or under a strong light, and leave to stand for at least a couple of hours. Ask an adult to cut the carrot lengthwise, so that you can see the interior.

What's happening? The carrot has absorbed the red water.

Coconut and chocolate

SERVES 2

1 banana

generous ¾ cup / 200 ml milk

7 tbsp / 100 ml coconut milk

3 tbsp O'boy or 1 tbsp cacao powder
+ 3 tbsp confectioner's sugar

2 tsp coconut flakes

3 scoops vanilla ice cream

4 ice cubes

coconut flakes or fresh-grated coconut
for the garnish

1. Peel and chop the banana, and place it in the blender.

2. Add the milk, coconut milk, O'boy or cacao with sugar, coconut flakes, and ice to the blender, and blend for a few seconds.

3. Add the ice cream and blend until you get an ice-cream-like smoothie.

4. Pour into glasses, sprinkling with a few coconut flakes or fresh-grated coconut.

MAKE YOUR OWN COCONUT MILK

Coconut milk is made from the shredded flesh of the coconut, which is blended with water and then squeezed. Making your own coconut milk is not at all difficult. Combine the scraped and shredded coconut flesh with water in a blender, and blend for a long while, until the mixture becomes smooth. Then strain the mixture. And presto! You've just made your own coconut milk!

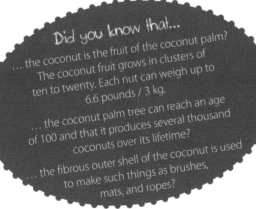

Did you know that...

... the coconut is the fruit of the coconut palm? The coconut fruit grows in clusters of ten to twenty. Each nut can weigh up to 6.6 pounds / 3 kg.

... the coconut palm tree can reach an age of 100 and that it produces several thousand coconuts over its lifetime?

... the fibrous outer shell of the coconut is used to make such things as brushes, mats, and ropes?

Blackcurrant and apple

SERVES 2

3 cups / 300 g blackcurrants, fresh or frozen

½ banana

generous ¾ cup / 200 ml fresh-pressed apple juice

Did you know that...

... if you smell the blackcurrant shrub, you will find that it gives off the same lovely perfume as the berries? You can use the leaves to make really good tea or a refreshing cold drink.

1. Wash all the fresh fruits thoroughly.

2. Remove the stems from the blackcurrants (if you use fresh ones) and place two thirds of the currants in the blender. Reserve the rest for the garnish.

3. Peel and slice the half banana and add to the blender.

4. Pour in the apple juice and blend it all to a smooth consistency. For an even smoother consistency, you can strain the smoothie before pouring it into glasses.

5. Pour into glasses and sprinkle the remaining blackcurrants on top.

6. Serve!

TIP
This smoothie will be a delicious breakfast if you blend in a generous ¾ cup / 210 g of Greek yogurt and 2 tsp of honey.

Orange and banana

2 bananas

3 oranges or 1¾ cups / 400 ml
fresh-pressed orange juice

½ lime

4 ice cubes

1. Wash all the fruits.

2. Peel and chop the bananas, and place them in the blender.

3. Juice the oranges and the lime half with a citrus press. Be sure to strain out all the pips as, otherwise, the smoothie will have a bitter taste.

4. Add the ice and blend it all to a smooth consistency.

5. Pour into glasses and serve with an apple slice.

TIP

A few strawberries would give this smoothie a lovely color and exciting flavor.

Did you know that...

... according to Guinness World Records the largest orange in the world was grown in California, USA, in 2006? It had a whopping 25 inch / 63.5 cm circumference (the width measured round the widest part of the fruit)?

... if you plant a single orange pip, you will probably find more than one plant growing from it?

Cherry and coconut

SERVES 2

generous 1 cup / 200 g cherries,
fresh or frozen

½ banana

2 wedges of lime

generous ¾ cup / 200 g vanilla quark

7 tbsp / 100 ml milk

3 tbsp coconut milk

1. Wash all the fresh fruits thoroughly.

2. Carefully pit the cherries, if you use fresh ones. Get help from an adult if you are finding it difficult. Place the cherries in the blender.

3. Peel and slice the half banana and add it to the blender.

4. Using your fingers, squeeze the juice of the 2 lime wedges into a small bowl. Strain out all the pips, otherwise the smoothie will have a bitter taste.

5. Add the lime juice, vanilla quark, milk, and coconut milk to the blender.

6. Blend it all to a smooth and viscous consistency.

7. Serve!

Experiment: How do you get bananas to ripen quickly?

For this experiment, you will need:

2 apples

3 green, unripe bananas

1 small paper or plastic bag

Method: Place the first banana with the apples in a paper or plastic bag, and close the bag. Place the second banana in a fruit bowl, making sure there is not any other fruit near. Place the third banana in the refrigerator. Wait for two days.

What's happened? The banana in the bag has become overripe. The banana in the fruit bowl is just ripe enough. The banana in the refrigerator is still unripe.

Why, you may ask. The banana in the bag ripened quickly because the apples gave off ethylene gas, which speeds up ripening. The one in the fridge did not ripen because of the cold.

Blueberry and banana

1 cup / 100 g blueberries, fresh or frozen

1 banana

7 tbsp / 100 ml fresh-pressed apple juice

generous ¾ cup / 200 g vanilla yogurt

2 tsp confectioner's sugar

4 ice cubes (if you use fresh blueberries)

1. Wash the blueberries thoroughly, if you use fresh ones, and leave to dry. Reserve a few for the garnish.

2. Peel, skin, and slice the banana, and place it in the blender.

3. Blend the banana, blueberries, apple juice, yogurt, and confectioner's sugar to a smooth consistency. Add ice cubes if you are using fresh blueberries.

4. Pour into glasses and serve with a few blueberries on a cocktail stick or toothpick.

TIP
Replace blueberries with other berries—e.g. strawberries, raspberries, blackberries, or blackcurrants.

Drying blueberries

You can dry blueberries yourself. Follow these steps. Spread pre-washed blueberries on a tray or cookie sheet, being careful not to overcrowd them, and let them air-dry indoors for a few days. Then, transfer them onto a cookie sheet into the oven, and dry at 122 °F / 50 °C. The drying time will depend on the water content, but it could take a few hours. The blueberries will be ready when they are fully dry. Consider leaving them to continue drying in an airy place for a while. Store dried berries in glass jars, in a dark place. You can dry lingonberries and cranberries in the same way. Sweet they sure are, but they are much better for you than candy!

Redcurrant and mango

SERVES 2

1 mango

2 cups / 200 g redcurrants, fresh or frozen

½ banana

7 tbsp / 100 ml ice-cold water

ice cubes (optional)

1. Wash all the fresh fruits thoroughly.

2. Peel the mango with a vegetable peeler and carefully chop it into small chunks. Keep in mind that there is a hard pit inside, so be extra careful. Get help from an adult if you are finding it difficult.

3. Place the mango chunks in the blender.

4. Remove the stems from the redcurrants (if you use fresh ones) and add them to the blender. You may want to reserve a couple of stems for the garnish.

5. Peel and slice the half banana and add to the blender.

6. Pour in the water and blend it all to a smooth consistency. For a frostier consistency, add a few ice cubes.

7. Serve decorated with a small bunch of redcurrants.

Did you know that...

... the redcurrant grows wild in western Europe and elsewhere, and is cultivated all over the world? You can use white currants, which taste the same. The only difference will be that your smoothie will not have the same nice color.

Raspberry and cinnamon

SERVES 2

1 banana

2 cups / 200 g raspberries, fresh or frozen

6 tbsp / 100 g Turkish/Greek yogurt

7 tbsp / 100 ml milk

2 tbsp runny honey

1 pinch cinnamon

4 ice cubes (if you use fresh raspberries)

1. Peel, skin, and slice the banana, and place it in the blender.

2. Wash the raspberries, if you use fresh ones, and leave them to dry. Reserve a few for the garnish.

3. Add the raspberries, yogurt, milk, honey, cinnamon, and ice cubes (if you use fresh raspberries) to the blender.

4. Blend it all to a smooth consistency.

5. Serve with a few raspberries.

Freezing raspberries

Raspberries are easy to freeze. However, be sure you do not freeze them in a clump, as they will turn mushy when they defrost. Spread them on a plate, leaving some space between the berries, and freeze. When they are individually frozen, scoop them into a jar and place them back in the freezer. They will be delicious during the winter months.

Almond chocolate with banana and vanilla

SERVES 2

2 bananas, fresh or frozen

1¾ cups / 400 ml almond milk (or 4 tsp almond butter + 1½ cups / 350 ml water)

4 dates, pitted

2 tbsp cacao powder

1 tsp vanilla sugar

a few ice cubes (if you use fresh bananas)

crushed almonds for the garnish

1. Wash, peel, and slice the bananas.

2. Place all the ingredients except the ice cubes in the blender and blend to a smooth consistency.

3. Blend in the ice cubes if you use fresh bananas and if you want a frosty smoothie.

4. Serve in pretty tumblers and sprinkle some crushed almonds on top.

Did you know that...

... almonds are usually referred to as nuts, but are actually a stone fruit? The almond nut is a seed nestled inside a hard outer shell.

... almonds contain lots of fiber and are particularly rich in vitamin E?

... even though you can buy unsweetened almond milk in a grocery store, you can easily make your own? The milk you make yourself will contain more almonds than the store-bought kind. Beware of ready-to-drink, sweetened almond milk as it contains lots of sugar.

What is a stone fruit?

A stone fruit is a juicy fruit that contains a single seed, called a pit or stone, inside a soft or hard, outer shell. Examples of these fruit include plums, apricots, cherries, almonds, and peaches. Even raspberries and blackberries are sometimes considered stone fruits because each drupelet seed is encased in fruity flesh.

Melon and passion fruit

½ honeydew melon (approx. 1½ cups / 300 g flesh)

4 passion fruit

½ banana

½ lime

7 tbsp / 100 ml fresh-pressed apple juice

a few slices of the melon as a snack

1. Wash all the fruits thoroughly.

2. Cut the melon in half, removing the seeds with an ice-cream scoop. Discard the seeds. Scoop out the flesh and place it in the blender.

3. Cut the passion fruit in half, remove the pulp, and add to the blender. You may want to reserve one passion fruit for the garnish.

4. Peel and slice the half banana and add to the blender.

5. Juice the half lime using a citrus press. Be sure to strain out all the pips as, otherwise, the smoothie will have a bitter taste.

6. Pour in the lime juice, apple juice, and water, and blend it all to a smooth consistency. If you like, you can strain the smoothie for a smoother consistency before serving.

7. Serve with a few melon slices.

TIP

The easiest way to separate the seeds of the passion fruit from the pulp is to pour a little water into each half and stir until all the pulp loosens. Strain, using only the tasty liquid in the smoothie.

For a showy effect, reserve one passion fruit for the garnish. Scoop out half a passion fruit and place it on top of each glass.

Blueberry, oat, and vanilla

1½ cups / 200 g blueberries, frozen

5 dates, pitted

1¾ cups / 400 ml oat milk

1 tsp vanilla sugar

1. Place all the ingredients in the blender and blend to a frosty consistency.

2. Serve in pretty tumblers and garnish with a few blueberries.

Make your own oat milk:

It is very easy to make oat milk yourself. Soak a generous ¾ cup / 80 g rolled oats for a few hours or overnight. Place the oats in the blender, along with 4 cups / 1 liter of water and a small pinch of salt, and blend until the oats have completely dissolved and the consistency has become milky. Strain using an extra-fine sieve or a nut milk bag (available from health food stores). Oat milk will keep in a glass bottle in the refrigerator for a couple of days.

Feel free to flavor your oat milk with a little cinnamon, cardamom, vanilla, cacao powder, or another suitable flavoring, and sweeten with honey, agave syrup, or dates. If you use spices or other flavorings, add them to the blender when you blend the oats with water. Then strain as usual.

The ABC of fruit

APPLE. Apples are high in vitamin C, antioxidants, and dietary fiber. Apples should be stored in a cool place, preferably in a plastic bag in the refrigerator, because they have a short shelf life at room temperature. They give off ethylene gas, which fosters ripening. Freshly picked apples have by far the best flavor. Apples keep well dried; just remove the core and slice them first.

APRICOT. The apricot has an exterior similar to that of a plum, but its skin is orange and slightly downy. Apricots contain beta-carotene, which is converted to vitamin A in the body. They also contain dietary fiber, vitamin C, and potassium. You can keep apricots for a day or two at room temperature, but they are best stored in the refrigerator.

BANANA. Green and unripe when they arrive here, bananas ripen with ethylene. They are high in potassium, vitamin B6, and magnesium. Bananas should always be stored at room temperature—preferably in their own bowl and away from other fruits. The chill of the refrigerator makes bananas turn black. They are sensitive to impact. If pressed, they quickly turn brown and their flesh gets damaged.

BLACKBERRY. Contains a lot of potassium and vitamin C, and very rich in fiber. If you want to get hold of tasty wild blackberries, it is important that you wait until they become ripe, usually in September or October. Cultivated blackberries can be picked earlier. Blackberries will keep for only one day at room temperature, but they freeze well.

BLUEBERRY. Contains large amounts of vitamin C, B, and antioxidants. Pick only blue ones, never those that are black, and wash them well. If you buy them in the store, try to find plump berries that are regular sized and not wrinkled. Blueberries keep for one or two days in the refrigerator, and freeze well. Stores sell American blueberries. They are bigger and taste fruitier than other varieties, and keep very well at cool refrigerator temperatures. However, they do not contain as many antioxidants as wild blueberries.

CARROT. When carrots reached Europe from Central Asia in the 12th century, they were bright red in color. Carrots contain beta-carotene, which is converted to vitamin A in the body and which gives them their orange-red color. Carrots are best stored in the refrigerator or a cool place, in a plastic bag without their greens. Be sure to cut off the greens as they sap nutrients from the root and make it soften.

CHERRY/ROYAL ANN CHERRY. Cherries can be subdivided into sweet and tart varieties. The Royal Ann cherry is a sweet variety high in vitamin C. Cherries also contain potassium and dietary fiber, and there is research to suggest that they have a certain anti-inflammatory effect. Look for firm, plump berries with unblemished, taut, and glossy skin, and an undamaged stalk. Cherries will keep for a few days at room temperature and for up to a couple of weeks in the refrigerator. They are sensitive to pressure and do not keep well in a bag.

CITRUS FRUITS. The generic name for a large number of fruits rich in vitamin C, including orange, clementine, lemon, grapefruit, lime, tangerine, and satsuma. All citrus fruits can be stored both at room temperature and in the refrigerator. Thin-skinned citrus becomes juicier if left at room temperature, whereas fruit with a thicker skin yields the most juice if stored cold.

CLEMENTINE, SATSUMA, and **TANGERINE.** Tangerines have a lot of pips and are therefore not a popular import. Clementines and satsumas are easy to peel and usually seedless. The skin of the satsuma has a green tinge although it is harvested ripe, like other citrus fruits.

COCONUT. The fruit of the coconut palm. It is an oval stone fruit, 8–12 inches (20–30 cm) long and weighing 4½ –6½ pounds (2–3 kg). The coconut has two outer shells: a leathery and a fibrous one. Inside these is the hard brown pit that is filled with coconut water, which gradually solidifies into coconut flesh. Coconut milk and coconut butter are prepared from the flesh. Coconut flakes are flesh that has been grated and dried. Fresh coconut is high in fiber (9%) and fat (33%), most of which is saturated fat. A coconut can be stored in the refrigerator for about five to six weeks.

DATES. Dates are stone fruits. Rich in fiber, potassium, and vitamins A and D, they are not sensitive to drying out and will keep for up to two months if stored at 32 °F (0 °C). They can be thawed and refrozen.

GOJI BERRY. A superberry that is good for the immune system. It has a flavor like that of a lingonberry or raisin. Do not eat more than a small handful of whole berries, or one teaspoon of goji powder, a day. Store in a dry, dark, and cool place. You should consume an opened package of dried goji berries within a couple of months.

GRAPEFRUIT. Half a grapefruit a day gives you more than your daily requirement of vitamin C. Grapefruit tastes fresh and aromatic, but also a little bitter. Choose fruits that are firm and intact. Its shelf life varies depending on the country it comes from. Grapefruit is best stored at a cool temperature, 50–60 °F (10–15 °C). Anyone with a cardiovascular problem should steer clear of grapefruit!

GRAPES. Grapes contain vitamin C, potassium, and dietary fiber. They are always harvested ripe and have a short shelf life. They should be eaten straightaway or stored in a plastic bag in the refrigerator, where they will keep for a week. They taste best if taken out of the refrigerator 20 minutes before being served.

KIWI. Kiwi is rich in vitamin C and potassium. Kiwis can be eaten with or without the skin. Green-fleshed fruit is the most common variety, but there are also yellow-fleshed kiwis that taste a little sweeter. The kiwi will ripen after a few days at room temperature, but you can speed up the process by placing the fruit in a plastic bag along with an apple. Unripe kiwis will keep for three weeks in the refrigerator if stored in a plastic bag. Throw away any fruit that is wrinkled or mushy. The fruit takes its name from the kiwi, a bird that is New Zealand's national symbol.

LIME. Lime is related to lemon and is used in the same way, but it has a slightly more rounded and aromatic flavor. Store limes in the vegetable drawer as they do not take kindly to frost.

LINGONBERRY. Lingonberries contain moderate amounts of calcium, iron, vitamin C, and vitamin E. They keep well in the refrigerator, in a

plastic box lined with paper towels. Stored like that, they will keep for a couple of weeks, and sometimes for up to a month. Lingonberries contain benzoic acid, which extends shelf life and helps to preserve raw lingonberries mixed with a small amount of sugar without preservatives. You can also freeze fresh berries.

MANGO. Mangoes contain carotene and antioxidants. Gently press the fruit to choose one that is ripe. The mango should give, but not be too soft. Another tip is to smell it. Unfortunately, you will not be able to tell whether it is ripe or not by the color of its skin, because there are more than a thousand known mango varieties with different colors. The mango will keep for up to two weeks in the refrigerator. It will ripen fast at room temperature if placed in a bag along with an apple or banana. Once ripe, mangos should be stored in the refrigerator for a few days at a temperature not lower than 50 °F (10 °C). Peeled and diced mango freezes well in freezer bags, but be sure to remove the pit first.

MELON. The melon is related to the pumpkin and the cucumber. Melons are subdivided into sweet melons and watermelons. The pips of the sweet melon are concentrated in the middle of the fruit, whereas those of the watermelon are dispersed throughout the flesh (more information available under 'watermelon'). Try smelling the melon before buying it. If you can smell a perfume at the blossom end (the one opposite the stem end), the melon is ripe. Uncut melons can be stored at room temperature, but should be placed in the refrigerator after you begin cutting them. Melons give off ethylene gas, which speeds up ripening.

ORANGE. All citrus fruits are rich in vitamin C. Watch out for the really large fruits as they usually have a watered-down taste. Instead, look for oranges that are heavy for their size and, preferably, those that have a thin, smooth skin. Oranges are best stored in plastic bags in the refrigerator, but will keep for a week or two at room temperature.

PAPAYA. Papaya contains vitamins A and C, and is eaten in the same way as the melon. Papaya is best stored in the refrigerator, where it will keep for up to three weeks. An unripe papaya can ripen within a few days at room temperature. Papaya has a yellow-green, inedible skin and orange flesh that is sweet and flavorsome. When ripe, the papaya should have an even color. Squeeze some lime over the flesh to intensify the flavor. Though edible, the seeds of the papaya are usually not eaten as they taste a little peppery and cannot easily be blended into smoothies or juices. You can freeze papaya if you peel it, remove the seeds, and cut it into chunks.

PASSION FRUIT. Passion fruit contains vitamin C, carotene, potassium, and dietary fiber. A common variety sold is the red-violet one, but there are also yellow and red-yellow varieties, which are a little larger. Passion fruit contains potassium and beta-carotene, among other nutrients. When buying passion fruit, make sure they are firm and a little wrinkled. They should not be too wrinkled as that means they are overripe. They should not be too light either as that indicates dryness inside. Passion fruit keep for three to four weeks in the refrigerator. The flesh freezes well—place it first in an ice-cube tray and then store the frozen pieces in an airtight freezer bag. Frozen cubes will keep for two to three months in the freezer and can be used as a garnish or an ingredient in fruit juices and smoothies.

PEACH. The peach contains A, B, and C vitamins. It ripens fast at room temperature and will keep for only one or two days. In the refrigerator, though, it will keep for up to two weeks. Peaches are best stored in a plastic bag, where they are protected from drying out. The nectarine is a variety of peach with a smooth skin. It usually has a more intense perfume than the peach.

PEAR. Pears have been cultivated for thousands of years. They contain potassium, vitamins A and C, and dietary fiber. Pears have a short shelf life and are best stored in a plastic bag in the refrigerator. If you want them to develop as much flavor as possible be sure to keep them at room temperature for one or two days before eating. Pears give off ethylene gas, which will make other fruit in the fruit bowl ripen faster.

PINEAPPLE. Very high in vitamin C. Try pulling off one of the outer leaves to check that the pineapple is ripe. If it pulls out easily, the fruit is ripe. Your safest bet is to buy an unripe pineapple and let it ripen at home. A ripe pineapple will keep for up to a week in the refrigerator and about three days at room temperature.

PLUM. Plums are rich in vitamin C and dietary fiber. The plum is a stone fruit and comes in a variety of different colors and sizes. Unripe plums will ripen in a few days at room temperature. Ripe plums are best stored in the refrigerator.

RASPBERRY. The variety most often available is the red one, but there are also yellow and black raspberries. Raspberries contain vitamin C and fiber, among other nutrients. The berries should be of an even color and should not be kept for any longer than two days in the refrigerator. Raspberries freeze well and will keep for two to three months when frozen.

REDCURRANT and **BLACKCURRANT.** Currants can be black, red, yellow, and white. Regardless of their color, they all contain vitamin C and dietary fiber. They will keep for two to three days at room temperature, and for approximately a week in the refrigerator. Currants freeze really well.

SEA BUCKTHORN. The sea buckthorn contains large amounts of vitamin C, as well as vitamin B12, which very rarely occurs in plants but is hugely important for vegetarians. Fresh berries will keep for a week in the refrigerator. Both berries and juice freeze well.

STRAWBERRY. Strawberries contain more vitamin C than oranges and are quite rich in iron. Strawberries are very sensitive to impact and easily turn bad if tightly packed. They may be refrigerated for a short time, but definitely taste best on the day they are picked. If freezing strawberries, either slice them and sprinkle a little sugar over them, or freeze them whole, but be sure to hull them first. Like most berries, they will keep for two to three months in the freezer.

WATERMELON. The watermelon contains vitamins A, B, and C. The most common variety has a green skin, but there are also varieties with green-speckled or yellow skin. The watermelon makes a very fine smoothie as it contains plenty of water. Choose firm watermelons, making sure you knock on them first. If they sound hollow, they are ripe. An uncut watermelon will keep up to 12 days at room temperature and even longer in the refrigerator.

Glossary

ANTIOXIDANT. A substance that protects against oxygen radicals (i.e. harmful substances produced in our cells when they use oxygen to extract energy). By eating a lot of fruits and vegetables you can make sure you get the antioxidants your body needs. The antioxidants that are especially beneficial are vitamin C, vitamin E, beta carotene, coenzyme Q10, and the trace element selenium.

BENZOIC ACID. Found in many fruits, berries, and vegetables, and acts as a natural preservative.

BETA-CAROTENE. A precursor to vitamin A. Found in carrots and kale, among other vegetables.

CAROTENES. Natural, yellow to yellow-red pigments found in carrots, mangoes, papaya and egg yolk, among others.

CELL. The smallest building block of all living things. Most cells are very small and are visible only under a microscope. There are many billions of cells in a body.

DIETARY FIBER. Found mainly in fruit, vegetables, and cereals. If the food you eat is high in fiber, it will move quickly through your gut, making you less likely to get constipated.

ENZYMES. Proteins needed to help trigger chemical reactions in the body. For example, you need the myosin enzyme for your muscles to contract when you want to move. Another example is pepsin, which breaks down proteins in the food we eat. Enzymes are essential for all organisms, and they are also used in detergents to dissolve certain stains.

ETHYLENE GAS. Some fruits and vegetables give off ethylene, a gas that speeds up the ripening process. It makes either an individual fruit or fruits and vegetables placed in the same bowl or bag ripen faster. Apples, pears, melons, bananas, peaches, nectarines, plums, apricots, and tomatoes give off a lot of ethylene gas, so they should not be stored close to other fruits and vegetables.

LACTOSE INTOLERANCE. If you are lactose intolerant, you do not have the lactase enzyme in your small intestine and you will find it difficult to digest milk and dairy products. Some people with lactose intolerance can eat sour milk and yogurt because they contain less lactose than regular, fresh milk. People with lactose intolerance usually get diarrhea and intestinal gas when they eat dairy foods. Lactose is also called milk sugar.

MINERALS. The human body needs about twenty different minerals, but only in very small quantities. The mineral we need most of is calcium, which is found in our bones and teeth. Other examples of essential minerals are phosphorus, potassium, sodium, and magnesium. Substances that we need only a minuscule amount of are called trace elements. They include iron, iodine, zinc, and selenium. The easiest way to make sure you get enough of all minerals is to eat a varied diet.

ORGANIC FARMING. Organic farmers do not use any chemical (or commercial) fertilizers or chemical agents. Farming that is not organic is called conventional farming.

OXIDATION. A chemical reaction. When you see a wedge of an apple go dark, that means that the chemicals in the apple are oxidizing because of the oxygen in the air.

PRESERVATIVES. Substances that extend shelf life. For example, preservatives added to foods prevent mold and fermentation.

VITAMINS. Vitamins are vital to life, but we need them only in small quantities. You will get all the vitamins your body needs by eating a balanced diet. To be on the safe side, though, many people like to take a vitamin pill every day. You will become sick if you are not getting enough of a vitamin. Humans need 12 different vitamins. They are usually subdivided into fat-soluble and water-soluble vitamins. The fat-soluble ones are vitamins A, D, E, and K. The water-soluble ones are the various vitamins in the vitamin B family (B1, B2, B6, B12, niacin, folic acid, biotin) and vitamin C. Vitamin A is needed for healthy eyesight and good immunity. Vitamin D is essential for strong bones. Vitamin E fights free radicals, for example. Vitamin K is needed for your blood to coagulate (change to a solid state) when you injure yourself. Vitamin C is also called ascorbic acid, and it helps the body to form connective tissue and to absorb iron from food. Vitamin C is good for immunity. It is most plentiful in fruit, berries, and vegetables.

Index